Waiting For You

To my daughter Ophelia. You are the wind in my sails and my guiding light in the darkness. You have opened my eyes and captured my heart. You give me courage and strength to keep moving forward. I will always love you.

How could it be, that I
never knew.
I've been waiting my whole
life for you.

I thank God everyday, to him I give the glory.
For designing a very special angel just for me.

Your rosy cheeks and
crooked smile,
make me stop and stay
awhile.

Nothing can match the
way you laugh.
When you're in the bath
and you splish and splash.

The sound of your name,
brings joy to my heart.
No matter what, we will
never be apart.

And if you ever wonder,
just how much I care.
Turn around darling,
and I'll be there.

Like the stars in the sky,
such a beautiful sight.
When you close your eyes
and kiss me goodnight.

Your little hand, holding
onto mine.
I won't let go, not till' the
end of time.

CPSIA information can be obtained
at www.ICGtesting.com
Printed in the USA
LVHW070922310821
696552LV00002B/16